The Hero's Journey Of Odysseus

A Monomyth Guide to the Iliad and Odyssey

By Josh Coker

Copyright

Copyright © 2017 by Story Ninjas

All rights reserved. This book or any portion thereof may not be reproduced or used in any manner whatsoever without the express written permission of the publisher, except for the use of brief quotations in a book review.

Table of Contents

Copyright	1
Table of Contents	2
Introduction	4
What is the Monomyth?	4
How is the Hero's Journey Structured?	7
Three Main Acts	7
17 Classic Stages	9
Archetypes	10
Recap	11
THE ILIAD	12
ACT 1: SEPARATION	13
Purpose of the Separation Act	13
Separation Stages	14
Recap	22
THE ODYSSEY	24
ACT 2: INITIATION	25
Purpose of the Initiation Act	25
Initiation Stages	26
Recap	39
ACT 3: THE RETURN	41
Purpose of the Return Act	42
Return Stages	42
Recap	53
Selected Bibliography	54
About Story Ninjas	55

About The Author 57

Introduction

The story of Odysseus is a model representation of Joseph Campbell's Monomyth. This guide will demonstrate how Odysseus' adventures perfectly match with the stages of the Hero's Journey.

The Greek mythological character Odysseus is one of the most revered heroes of all time. He was a king, a warrior, a strategist, a husband and a father. Not only did he fight in the Trojan war, but he also faced nymphs, witches, cyclops and gods. His epic adventures have been passed down for generations.

One might wonder what makes his story and character so different from the countless others which were forgotten in time.

The reason is explained by the Monomyth.

What is the Monomyth?

The term "Monomyth" comes from the Greek. It is broken into two root words: 1) mono, meaning "one", and 2) mythos, meaning "story." The connotation being, the "One Story." This term was coined by author James Joyce in his most famous work, *Ulysses* (the Roman name for Odysseus). However, it wasn't popularized until the late 1940's when a comparative mythologist by the name of Joseph Campbell, published his seminal work, *The Hero With A Thousand Faces*. In his book, Campbell suggested that there are common aspects that nearly all myths throughout time have shared. These elements combine into narrative format that can be used as an approach to mythology. Many people associate the "Hero's Journey" as synonymous with The Monomyth. Both, historical and modern storytellers have used it as an approach to analyze narratives and develop new plots and characters for contemporary audiences. According to Campbell, the Monomyth follows a three act structure. In the first act, The Separation, a hero is called to adventure and leaves his known world for the unknown world, guided by a mentor. Once the hero crosses the threshold of adventure, they enter the second act, The Initiation. In this section, the hero faces many tests and trials, confronts his inner demons (many times represented as ghosts, monsters, minotaurs, or dragons), then goes on through stages of enlightenment. Once the hero retrieves the boon, he must return it to the normal world from which he came. This third act is called the Return. During this final section of the narrative, the hero must release the power of the boon into society in order to restore it. Many times this last act requires the hero to overcome his major flaw and make a sacrifice. Once restored, the hero and those citizens in the world are free once again to live in it.

    The story of Odysseus follows this format very close. Particularly, if we combine the events from the Iliad and the Odyssey we obtain a full picture of Odysseus' journey of kingship.

How is the Hero's Journey Structured?

On a basic level, the Hero's Journey is broken into a three act structure. Within those acts, Joseph Campbell identified 17 specific stages. Since this is a basic overview, we will only look at the stages.

Three Main Acts

The three main acts are:
1. Separation
2. Initiation
3. Return

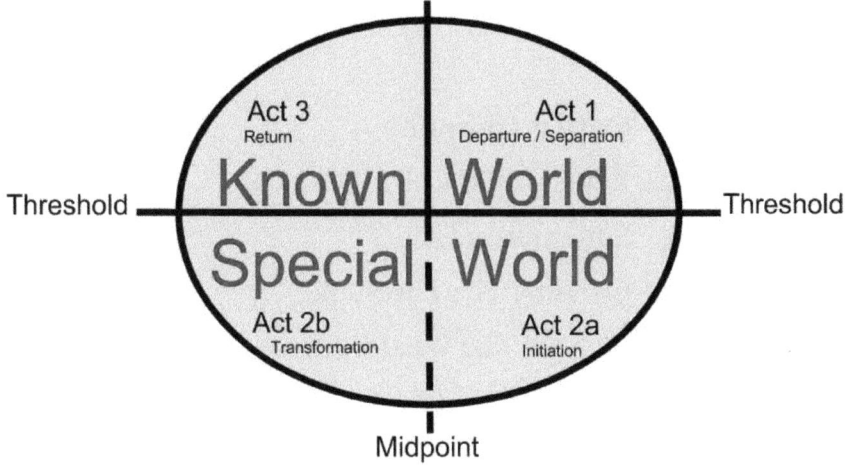

In the first act of Separation, the hero must leave his normal world behind by accepting the call to adventure, meeting helpers/mentors, and crossing the threshold into the special world. During the second act of Initiation, the hero must face the road of trials, approach the innermost cave, face death, and receive the ultimate boon. In the last act of the Return, the hero must go back to the normal world to share the boon with society. Normally this culminates in a final climax or battle, where the hero uses all that he's learned along the journey to win the day.

17 Classic Stages

There are 17 distinct classic stages that Joseph Campbell identified. They are listed below:

1. Call To Adventure
2. Refusal Of Call
3. Supernatural Aid
4. Crossing The Threshold
5. Belly Of The Whale
6. The Road Of Trials
7. Meeting With The Goddess
8. Woman as Temptress
9. Atonement With The Father
10. Apotheosis
11. Retrieve The Ultimate Boon
12. Refusal Of The Return
13. The Magic Flight
14. Rescue from Without
15. The Crossing Of The Return Threshold
16. Master Of Both Worlds
17. Freedom To Live

Archetypes

Aside from the three main plot events and 18 stages, the Monomyth is also comprised of several archetypes. These are characters that fulfill major roles in the story and represent a psychological forms that all humans recognize on a subconscious level. The hero, mentor, and shadow are just a few of the basic archetypes that comprise the Monomyth. As modern examples, Gandalf, Obi Wan, and Dumbledore are the epitome of the mentor archetype. While archetypes are critical to the Monomyth, they do not fit the scope of this book. If you wish to learn more about archetypes, please refer to my other books, courses and videos on the subject.

Now that we've discussed the basics of the Monomyth, let's do a quick recap before we look at Odysseus' Journey.

Recap

- Monomyth means the "one story"
- Elements of the Monomyth can be found in nearly all forms of mythology and fairy tales from around the world
- It's comprised of a three act structure
- There are 17 classic stages
- Utilizes psychological archetypes
- Many writers use it as an approach to narratives

Now that we've discussed the basics of the Monomyth, let's look at Odysseus' Journey. Particularly, we'll start with the Iliad.

THE ILIAD

The Iliad covers the beginning of Odysseus's journey. While Achilles is the main hero depicted in the majority of this narrative, Odysseus begins to take center stage after Achilles death. The Iliad explains the beginnings of the Greek-Trojan war and how our hero got involved. Since the story begins in media res (meaning in the middle, usually at a point of action or conflict) we must piece together what has transpired prior to the opening scenes. At the beginning of the journey, Odysseus is called from his Kingdom home of Ithaca and sent to fight alongside other Greek chieftains such as Agamemnon Menelaus, Achilles, Patroclus and Ajax--to name a few. After gathering forces, they raid the shores of Troy and fight in many battles against King Priam and his son Hector, the commander of the Trojan forces. For a long time the Greeks seem to be fighting a losing battle, and almost decide to give up. However, thanks to advice from the goddess Athena and a clever trick Odysseus comes up with, they are able to gain the upper hand in the war and defeat the Trojans once and for all.

ACT 1

SEPARATION

As mentioned previously, we will dissect each act of the Hero's Journey. We will break it down into core components, which are the stages. First the hero must leave his normal world by accepting the call to adventure, meeting helpers/mentors, and cross the threshold into the special world. In this chapter, we'll discuss the Separation Act of the Monomyth as it relates to the Iliad. Remember, the Hero's Journey is broken up into three main acts: Separation (also known as departure), Initiation (also know as trials/tests), and the Return.

Purpose of the Separation Act

In most Greek stories, this act a introduces us to a kingly hero (Odysseus) who is living in a mundane world (or known world) when he receives a call to adventure. Shortly after he comes in contact with a mentor (Athena), then crosses the threshold of the known world, for the unknown world (also known as the special world). Here on the brink of both worlds, he will experience his first taste of death.

Separation Stages

There are five classic stages in the Separation Act. Below is a list for easy reference:

1. Call to Adventure
2. Refusal of Call
3. Supernatural Aid
4. Crossing the Threshold
5. Belly of the Whale

In the following pages we'll analyze these stages in more detail.

The Call To Adventure

In this stage, the hero is in their natural habitat, going through their daily rituals. We are introduced to the world the hero lives in, rules he abides by. Most heroes start out with fairly ordinary strengths and skills compared to their peers, because they are untested. This stage gives the hero an initial mission. This normally is conveyed through the herald archetype who approaches the hero and tells them to go on a journey. Other times a hero is forced into a situation that is beyond their control. While this task may seem insignificant at the time, it will force the hero to come in contact with the mentor and eventually commit him to the overall journey.

The first stage in Odysseus' Journey, The Call To Adventure, can be pieced together from events in the Iliad and the Odyssey. Odysseus is living in his normal world as King of Ithaca. He is the son of King Laertes and grandson of the Messenger God, Hermes. As a demi-god-king, favored by the gods, and a master tactician, Odysseus is a prideful man. This inner flaw ends up causing him problems later down the road. Odysseus is married to Queen Penelope who is loyal, loving, and clever like her husband. When the war begins Odysseus is entering fatherhood. Penelope recently gave birth to his son, Telemachus. Unbeknownst to Odysseus, the Trojan prince Paris has "stolen" Helen, wife of Menelaus (and sister in law to Agamemnon--head chieftain of the Achaeans) and taken her back to Troy. Shortly after, Greek emissaries arrive in Ithaca and urge Odysseus to join them in a battle against the Trojans. These heralds provide the hero with the call to adventure.

The Refusal Of The Call

In this stage the hero refuses the call. This is a vital step in humanizing the hero. Psychologically speaking, flaws make the hero more relatable to the audience. When faced with change, the initial human reaction is to fight against it. Once the hero refuses, they normally go through a period of boredom or setbacks, which "punish" the hero for their resistance to the adventure. Eventually the situation gets so bad that the hero either changes their mind, or is forced to go on the journey.

In the second stage, The Refusal Of The Call, Odysseus disguises himself at first, hoping the emissaries will leave. His son, Telemachus is newly born and his fatherly instincts advise him to stay in Ithaca. Eventually Odysseus reveals himself to the emissaries and chastises the the heralds for bringing him this news. Nevertheless, he recognizes his duty as King of Ithaca and agrees to join the other Greek chieftains in the war against the Trojans.

Meeting The Supernatural Aid

In this stage the hero accepts the call, either because they are forced to out of boredom, or necessity. Once they've accepted the call, a mentor will come into the story in order to help them along the way. In mythology, this individual often had magical powers, so they were considered a "supernatural aid." Mentors are individuals who have been to the special world and can impart their wisdom on the hero. The mentor's job is to prepare the hero for the special world. They will provide tools and information that will assist the hero on the journey. In many cases the mentor also provides a psychological center for the hero to stay inwardly grounded when facing internal challenges.

In the third stage of Odysseus' Journey, Meeting The Supernatural Aid, we meet Athena,

Goddess of wisdom. On orders from her parents Zeus and Hera, Athena assists the Greeks throughout the Trojan war.

"But quickly, order Athena down to battle now, into the killing-ground of Trojans and Achaeans- and see that the Trojans break the sworn truce first and trample on the Argives in their triumph!" (4.076-4.084)

Odysseus in particular prays to the Goddess Athena for her help and protection before his night raid on the Trojans. While Athena does not directly interact with Odysseus in this scene, it is implied that she watches over him. Later in his adventures Athena assists both Odysseus and his son, Telemachus along both of their journeys by providing tools, tips, and help. Note: Interestingly enough, Athena sometimes takes the form of Mentor, whose name was later adopted to describe a teacher that acts in a "mentor" role. The character Mentor was a loyal follower of Odysseus who takes Telemachus under his wing while the king is away fighting the Trojans.

Crossing The Threshold

At this point in the journey, the hero finally sets out on the adventure. He will meet several threshold guardians. Each one will test the hero. Some will become friends or allies, while others will become rivals or enemies. The closer he gets to the threshold of adventure, the less familiar things are. By the time he crosses it, he is in a completely unknown or unexplored area, commonly referred to as the special world (also known as the unknown world, or the adventure world). This is a place that contrasts with the normal world where the hero started out. It has different rules and sometimes physics, which causes the hero to feel disoriented upon arrival.

Odysseus enters into stage four, Crossing The Threshold by setting sail for the shores of Troy. Odysseus and his men are joined by other warriors and chieftains of the Greek armada such as Agamemnon, Menelaus, Achilles, Patroclus and Ajax. The Greeks make attempts to leave port the winds cause major difficulties. The priests inform Agamemnon that the goddess Artemis is not pleased with them, and desires a sacrifice. Agamemnon's daughter to be exact. While he resists at first, the

Greek Chieftain ultimately is convinced by Menelaus and sacrifices his daughter. Artemis relents her winds and the armada sets sail for Troy.

The Belly Of The Whale

The belly of the whale marks the hero's first taste of death. In this stage the hero faces the enemy head on, but has no idea how to fight them. They are foreign to him and their tactics are exotic. He is untested in this new world and therefore he and his team will suffer for their lack of knowledge. Therefore they experience a major loss, usually death for the first time.

In the fifth, and final stage of the first act, The Belly Of The Whale, The Greeks reach the shores of Troy, where trench battles ensue against Hector and the Trojan army. For several years the Greeks fight the Trojans and nearly lose. The Trojan walls are impenetrable. Their fighting tactics are not the same that the Greeks faced in past battles. They lose many men in these battles, which dampens the army's moral. Many of the men attempt to abandon the campaign. Not to mention Agamemnon and Achilles constantly argue, causing discord among the men.

Eventually Odysseus devises a plan to use a giant wooden horse as a ploy to get into Priam's Kingdom. His trick works and the Trojans allow a small group of Greeks into their territory. In the end the Greeks defeat the Trojans, but not without heavy losses on both sides. Patroclus, Ajax, Hector, and Achilles (to name a few) all perish during the war.

    The hero Achilles was as great a fighter as Odysseus is a tactician. Before his death, Achilles states, *"Fate is the same for the man who holds back, the same if he fights hard. We are all held in a single honour, the brave with the weaklings. A man dies still if he has done nothing, as one who has done much."* (9.318-320) The Trojan War served as Odysseus' first true taste of death along his journey.

Recap

Just to recap, the separation act is where we meet the hero in their normal world and learn about their flaws, problems, and motives. We are introduced to their sidekicks, rivals, and mentors. The hero receives a call to adventure and shortly after, meets a mentor or guide who gives them tools and information for the journey ahead. As the hero sets out toward the special world, they face multiple threshold guardians that try to prevent them from crossing the threshold of adventure. Once they cross the threshold, they are normally swallowed up into the "belly of the whale," where they get their first taste of death, and are baptized into the special world. Throughout this act, the hero meets several characters, including sidekicks, heralds, mentors, threshold guardians, and antagonistic forces.

Now that we've discussed the Separation act of Odysseus' journey, let's look at the second act of Initiation which starts in The Odyssey.

THE ODYSSEY

The Odyssey covers the second and third act of Odysseus' journey. After winning the Trojan War and losing comrades in arms along the way (Achilles in particular) Odysseus and his men start their journey back to Ithaca. However, many forces are against the team of warriors and they are tested many times. They face witches, sirens, cyclops and scylla on their adventure. Moreover, Odysseus pride inadvertently incurs the wrath of Poseidon. Ultimately Odysseus alone is able to reach the shores of his homeland. Even then, he must prove himself to his wife and son, then confront the suitors before he can reclaim his throne.

ACT 2

INITIATION

As you already know, the Hero's Journey is broken up into three main acts, 1) Separation, 2) Initiation, and 3) Return. In this section, we will discuss the "Initiation" act of the Odysseus' Journey. This is where the hero sets out into the special world. He faces obstacles and learns new lessons, which will help him defeat the antagonistic force. He will also encounter several new people along the way.

Purpose of the Initiation Act

In many ways, the Initiation Act is the most exciting. Not only is this where most of the action happens, but it serves as a testing ground for the hero and his allies. The purpose of the Initiation Act is to test the hero and their allies with multiple obstacles that gradually build in difficulty over time. It introduces more key characters such as the shapeshifter, trickster, and shadow. The hero will get their first glimpse of the special world, and its difficulties. The hero experiences death and sacrifice on a much deeper level than he did in the separation act. In the first half of the Initiation stage, the hero must face a series of tests that teach him valuable lessons about the special world. After these trials he will go through the transformative stages in order to find balance in his life. According to Joseph Campbell, ancient myths had four types of transformations: 1) meeting with the goddess, 2) atonement with the father, 3) apotheosis, and 4) the ultimate boon. In modern stories we normally see the hero go through all of these stages or a variation of them.

Initiation Stages

There are six classic stages in the Initiation Act. Below is a list for easy reference (continuing from the Separation Act):

1. The road of Trials
2. Meeting with the Goddess
3. Temptation

4. Atonement with the Father
5. Apotheosis
6. Retrieve the Ultimate Boon

In the following pages we'll analyze these stages in more detail.

The Road Of Trials

After leaving the belly of the whale, the hero will be completely immersed in the special world and fully on their journey. During the road of trials, the hero will be on the run from the antagonistic force. This will entail running, hiding, licking wounds, seeking shelter, and trying to catch their breath. Along the path, the hero will meet more threshold guardians like ogres, goblins, dragons, monsters, and dark nights. Many times the heroes must face difficult terrain along the road of trials. This could be quicksand, high cliffs, dark caves, crashing waves, asteroids, and several other obstacles. The point of these trials is to teach the hero the lessons needed to complete the journey. This stage normally is the longest and most episodic of the story.

The second act starts out with stage six, The Road Of Trials. During this stage, the war is over and Odysseus is ready to return to Ithaca. "*...what I want and all my days I pine for is to go back to my house and see my day of homecoming. And if some god batters me far out on the wine-blue water, I will endure it, keeping a stubborn spirit inside me, for already I have suffered much and done much hard* *work on the waves and in the fighting. So let this adventure follow."* (5.219-224) On their way back, he and his men pillage the land of the Cicones. Later they go to the island of the lotus eaters where they must overcome medicinal flowers. *"My men went on and presently met the Lotus-Eaters, nor did these Lotus-Eaters have any thoughts of destroying our companions, but they only gave them lotus to taste of. But any of them who ate the honey-sweet fruit of lotus was unwilling to take any message back, or to go away, but they wanted to stay there with the lotus-eating people, feeding on lotus, and forget the way home."* (9.91-97) After that they face Polyphemus, the cyclops and use a giant beam to poke his eye out. *"...I told the rest of the men to cast lots, to find out which of them must endure with me to take up the great beam and spin it in the Cyclops' eye when sweet sleep had come over him. The ones drew it whom I myself would have wanted chosen, four men, and I myself was the fifth, and allotted with them."* (9.331-335) Once blinded, Odysseus taunts the one eyed monster by saying, *"Cyclops, in the end it was no weak man's companions you were to eat by violence and force in your hollow cave, and your evil deeds were to catch up with you, and be too strong for you, hard one, who dared to eat your own guests in your own house, so Zeus and the rest of the gods have punished you."* (9.475-479) While they defeat the creature by tricking him, Odysseus' pride gets the best of him and he inadvertently incurs the wrath of Polyphemus father, Poseidon. When they leave, Odysseus boasts, *"Cyclops, if any mortal man ever asks you who it was that inflicted upon your eye this shameful blinding, tell him that you were blinded by Odysseus, sacker of cities. Laertes is his father, and he makes his home on Ithaka."* (9.500-505) They nearly make it back to Ithaca, when his men open a bag of magical winds which sends Odysseus and his crew even further than where they started. *"Nevertheless we sailed on, night and day, for nine days, and on the tenth at last appeared the land of our fathers, and we could see people tending fires, we were very close to them. But then the sweet sleep came upon me, for I was worn out with always handling the sheet myself, and I could not give it to any other companion, so we could come home quicker to our own country; but my companions talked with each other and said that I was bringing silver and gold home with me, given me by great-hearted Aiolos, son of Hippotas; ... and the evil counsel of my companions prevailed, and they opened the bag and the winds all burst out. Suddenly the storm caught them away and swept them over the water weeping, away from their own country."* (10.28-36, 46-49) After that, they head for the land of the Laestrygonians, a place filled with giants. They anger the giants and ultimately lose their ship.

Meeting With The Goddess

In this stage, the hero encounters a divine being with godlike power. The purpose of the divine is for the hero to find balance in himself. In ancient myths, the combination of the masculine energy and the feminine energy represented completeness and godliness. If the divine is a goddess, they are usually depicted as a mother, sister, or lover figure. Even after the road of trials stage comes to an end, the hero and team still must face various trials, tests, and threshold guardians to reach the goddess. This divine character represents the power of femininity, which is the power of life and death, or good and evil. The divine character is extremely similar to the mentor, in the sense that they provide the hero with more information and tools that will help them with the latter half of the journey. However, the goddess figure normally is more powerful than the mentor and gives more effective tools to the hero.

Stage seven, Meeting With The Goddess, starts when Odysseus and his men arrive on Circe's island. *"So she spoke to them, and the rest gave voice, and called her and at once she opened the shining doors, and came out, and invited them in, and all in their innocence entered; only Eurylochus waited outside, for he suspected treachery. She brought them inside and seated them on chairs and benches, and mixed them a potion, with barley and cheese and pale honey added to Pramnian wine, but put into the mixture malignant drugs, to make them forgetful of their own country. When she had given them this and they had drunk it down, next thing she struck them with her wand and drove them into her pig pens, and they took on the look of pigs, with the heads and voices and bristles of pigs, but the minds within them stayed as they had been before."* (10.229-241) The magical witch turns his men into pigs. But Odysseus, guided by the advice of his grandfather, the god

Hermes, is able to withstand her magic by eating the root of a plant. Having passed Circe's test, the hero earns her approval, adoration, and allegiance. *"Come then, goddess, answer me truthfully this: is there some way for me to escape away from deadly Charybdis, but yet fight the other off, when she attacks my companions?" 'So I spoke, and she, shining among goddesses, answered: "Hardy man, your mind is full forever of fighting and battle work. Will you not give way even to the immortals? She is no mortal thing but a mischief immortal, dangerous, difficult and bloodthirsty, and there is no fighting against her, nor any force of defense. It is best to run away from her."* (12.112-120)

Woman as Temptress

In this stage, the hero faces a major temptation that threatens to lure him away from the journey. In old Arthurian myths, this was normally a woman that would tempt a knight from completing his quest. However, this stage can be any type of temptation from any type of character as long as it fits the theme of the story. Sexual temptation, greed, power, or breaking one's ethics are all examples of temptation motifs. While there may be several temptations throughout the story, this one normally happens near the midpoint and tries to take the hero away from the journey. Keep in mind, the hero's team mates can be affected by this temptation too.

This is section is followed by stage eight, Woman as Temptress, where Circe makes advances towards Odysseus. The hero concedes, under the condition that she free his men. After this Circe advises Odysseus on a ritual which will allow him to enter the underworld, ultimately allowing culminating in the approach of the innermost cave.

Atonement With The Father

This stage is very similar to the previous one. Again the hero comes in contact with a powerful being. Often, this figure is represented as a ghost, god, monster, shadow, dragon, minotaur, or some other creature that evokes fear. The purpose of this stage is for the hero to understand the power of the gods. That is, that death, and pain, and all of the atrocities of life are natural, and normal. Despite the ugliness and unfairness of life, it is far beyond the judgement of mortals. The hero must realize this, and understand that they have no power over the horrific world they live in, and that they too are a monster in their own right, inflicting both life and death on the world. This stage generally marks the crisis, or midpoint of the story.

The ninth stage, Atonement With The Father, is where Odysseus travels to the underworld. Using the methods of sacrifice Circe advised him on, the hero descends into the dark underworld. There he encounters ghosts of old friends, including one of his lost sailors, the hero Achilles, and many others. *"Aias, son of stately Telamon, could you then never even in death forget your anger against me, because of that cursed armor? The gods made it to pain the Achaians, so great a bulwark were you, who were lost to them. We Achaians grieved for your death as incessantly as for Achilleus the son of Peleus at his death, and there is no other to blame, but Zeus; he, in his terrible hate for the army of the Danaan spearmen, visited this destruction upon you."* (11.553-560)

He also speaks with his dead mother. "*Mother, why will you not wait for me, when I am trying to hold you, so that even in Hades' with our arms *embracing we can both take the satisfaction of dismal mourning? Or are you nothing but an image that proud Persephone sent my way, to make me grieve all the more for sorrow?"* (11.210-214)

Apotheosis

In this stage, the hero experiences momentary godhood, or "apotheosis." In order to do that, most heroes must first go through an apostasis, that is, a dismemberment or removal of their old self. This can be a body part, weapon, tool, belief, a member of their team, or even someone from their past (or a variation). This removal serves as a sacrifice of the old self, making the hero vulnerable. This allows the hero to find balance within himself and start to heal. The hero realizes their own divinity for the first time. The hero is able to enter a state of godliness and wield a godlike power on a level only the divine can control. This will be their first taste of the divine power that resides within them. From this point on, the hero will continually tap into the inner truth they've been missing, making them more and more powerful. By the climax, the hero will have the power to completely tap into this divine power and defeat the antagonistic force.

The tenth stage, Apotheosis takes place simultaneously with the previous stage. Odysseus momentarily achieves the godlike power to descend to the underworld and commune with the dead friends and family he's lost along his journey. This is not a feat any mere mortal could achieve.

Retrieve The Ultimate Boon

The ultimate boon is an item of utmost importance to the story. Sometimes the boon is a reward, or information. Other times it is an artifact of great power, or a weapon. And sometimes it can even be a healing elixir. Unlike other weapons, tools, and artifacts in the story, the boon symbolically represents a key aspect of the theme. In several stories, there is a physical boon, and a metaphysical boon. Other times, there are two opposing boons which represent the dichotomy of life. Many times the divine figure from Stage 7 (Circe) is the person who sends the hero on a quest to retrieve this boon. The hero and their team believe the mission to be an impossible task because it requires them to approach the innermost cave and face the god-like parental figure.

In the Odyssey Stage eleven, Retrieve The Ultimate Boon, happens at the culmination of his discussions with the ghosts in the underworld. Odysseus learns of Poseidon's anger, and is told that he must make amends with the god of the sea if he is to ever reach Ithaca again. The ghosts also provide information on how to get back home. Additionally, Achilles gives Odysseus insight into overcoming his psychological flaw (pride), by telling the hero that he wished he had lived a normal life, rather than going to war and ending up the king of the dead in the underworld.

Recap

As mentioned earlier, the Initiation Act serves as a testing ground for the hero and his allies. The purpose of the Initiation Act is to test the hero and the team with multiple obstacles that gradually build in difficulty over time. It introduces key characters such as the shapeshifter, trickster, and the shadow. The hero will get their first glimpse of the special world, and its difficulties. The hero experiences death and sacrifice on a much deeper level than he did in the Separation Act. The Initiation Act is split into two sections: trials and transformation. During the trials the hero will face a series of tests that teach him valuable lessons. After these trials, the hero will go through the transformative stages in order to find balance in his life and reach his full potential. At the end of this act, either the hero or the shadow will have taken possession of the boon.

Now that we've covered the Initiation act of Odysseus' Journey, let's take a look at the final act, The Return.

ACT 3

THE RETURN

During this act the hero will have to face the antagonistic force for the last time in a climactic battle. He will be tested once again, but the stakes will be much higher. He must use all of the lessons learned in the Initiation Act in order to achieve victory. Normally this requires a major sacrifice on the hero's part. In most cases the hero must overcome their major flaw, and in some cases this requires them to actually become a martyr for the cause. Only through death of the old self can the hero be reborn anew. Once the sacrifice is made, the hero reaches a divine state and has the power to revitalize the society. From that point, they have mastered both the ordinary world and the special world, bringing balance to both. Ultimately this frees the hero from fear of his past, and allows him to move on toward the future with boldness.

Purpose of the Return Act

In many ways, the Return Act is the most meaningful. Not only is this where the climax happens, but it provides the hero meaning to the journey and should deliver a lesson to the audience. The purpose of the Return Act is for the hero to bring the boon back to the normal world. It provides the hero's final test, normally in the form of a climactic battle, to prove he has retained all of the lessons in the narrative. The hero experiences death on the deepest level possible, which is martyrdom. Finally this act ties up loose ends and returns the hero back to the ordinary world, but with a renewed sense of purpose.

Return Stages

There are six classic stages in the Return Act. Below is a list for easy reference (continuing from the Initiation Act):

1. Refusal of the Return
2. The Magic Flight

3. Rescue from Without
4. The Crossing of the Return Threshold
5. Master of Two Worlds
6. Freedom to Live

In the following pages we'll analyze these stages in more detail.

Refusal Of The Return

This stage is similar to the Refusal of the Call, in that it shows an unwillingness on the hero's part to accept the change happening in his life. Having been in the special world for so long, the hero becomes accustomed to the new rules and does not desire to leave. Perhaps they have become addicted to their newfound powers, or lustful of new relationships, or fearful of what might happen if they go back. Or perhaps they find the normal world too boring compared to the adventure they have experienced. In any event, once again the refusal proves to the audience that your hero is still human and has the same psychological issues as we all do. In mythology, the refusal was a return to the normal world. Even now, this is the purest and most potent use of this metaphysical stage.

The third act begins with the twelfth stage, Refusal Of The Return. After returning from the underworld, Odysseus stays with Circe for a year. Eventually he and his men set sail once again for Ithaca. The first obstacle they face is the island of sirens, beautiful women that sing enticing songs. Odysseus was warned that they were dangerous creatures that caused shipwrecks. Luckily Circe counseled Odysseus and his men to cover their ears. Odysseus follows the witch's advice, except for himself. Instead, he had his men tie him to the bow of the ship, so he could hear their songs. The enchanting melodies made him yearn to stay with the sirens. They sing to him, "*Come this way, honored Odysseus, great glory of the Achaians, and stay your ship, so that you can listen here to our singing; for no one else has ever sailed past this place in his black ship until he has listened to the honey-sweet voice that issues from our lips; then goes on, well-pleased, knowing more than ever he did; for we know everything that the Argives and Trojans did and suffered in wide Troy through the gods' despite. Over all the generous earth we know everything that happens.*" (12.184-196)

The Magic Flight

Although sometimes depicted as actual flying vehicles, chariots, or carpets, this stage is actually better defined by the term "pursuit" or "evasion." Many times the hero and antagonist (Poseidon/Suitors) are racing against each other in order to return to the normal world. The "magic" can be special technology, or an ethereal transcendence, or sometimes a method that the hero cannot do himself (piloting a ship). However, the purest form is when the hero is pursued by attackers.

    After the sirens, the hero enters into stage thirteen, The Magic Flight. In this section, Odysseus and his crew must pass through the Scylla and Charybdis. Odysseus makes a tough decision to sacrifice six men instead of the whole crew, and they are able to distract the Scylla and pass through unscathed. *"Right in her doorway she (the Skylla) ate them up. They were screaming and reaching out their hands to me in this horrid encounter. That was the most pitiful scene that these eyes have looked on in my sufferings as I explored the routes over the water."* (12.256-259)

    Unfortunately, at his the next stop, his men disobey his orders and eat some of Helios' sheep, which in turn incurs the wrath of Zeus. Ultimately his ship is destroyed and all but Odysseus perish in the aftermath. The hero makes his way to an island where he his held captive by Calypso, a sea nymph. Overtakend by love, she pleas with Odysseus to marry her and become her immortal husband. "...*the gods brought me to the island Ogygia, where Kalypso lives, with ordered hair, a dread goddess, and she received me and loved me excessively and cared for me, and she promised to make me an immortal and all my days to be ageless, but never so could she win over the heart within me.*" (7.254-258) While the hero denies her advances, the minor goddess traps him on the island for several years.

Rescue from Without

Many times the hero needs assistance crossing the return threshold, usually because the hero is weak, injured, or otherwise incapable. This help normally comes from an unlikely character - usually someone the hero has taken for granted, underestimated, or considered beneath him. Oftentimes this can be a sidekick or ally who left during the refusal of the return, or perhaps someone the hero had an argument with. After receiving help, the hero learns humility, which is necessary to temper his pride.

In stage fourteen, Rescue from Without, Odysseus' grandfather, the god Hermes, convinces Calypso to release him. She begrudgingly complies.

However, while sailing back to Ithaca, the still angry Poseidon wrecks his ship. This time Odysseus finds himself in the unknown lands of the Phaeacians. After Odysseus reveals himself as the king of Ithaca and recounts his journey thus far, their king, Alkinoos comes to his aid and provides Odysseus a vessel to get back home. *"O great Alkinoös, pre-eminent among all people, there is a time for many words, and a time for sleeping; but if you insists of hearing me still, I would not begrudge you the tale of these happenings and others yet more pitiful to hear, the sorrows of my companions, who perished later, who escaped the onslaught and cry of battle, but perished all for the sake of a vile woman, on the homeward journey."* (11.378-384) This act enrages Poseidon again, and this time he takes his anger out on the Phaeacians destroying their ships. After this fit of rage, the sea god is satisfied with his punishments and decides to stop tormenting Odysseus from that point on.

The Crossing Of The Return Threshold

Once the hero has returned, they must learn how to integrate their new knowledge into the normal world. This normally means fighting through more obstacles, which build and build until they culminate in the final climax. Everything leads the hero toward facing their enemy one last time in an epic battle/fight/argument at the climax of the narrative. Many times, crossing the return threshold causes heavy casualties for the hero and his team. Friends may be lost or killed in battle. By the end of this stage, the hero must face the enemy head on.

After almost 20 years along the journey, Odysseus reaches the fifteenth stage, The Crossing Of The Return Threshold. Once returning to Ithaca's shores, Odysseus must disguise himself from the suitors attempting to win his wife's hand in marriage. This act demonstrates that he has learned humility on his journey and is not as prideful as when he started out. Additionally, he must prove himself to his now adult son, Telemachus and then his wife Penelope. Since all of his men were killed in battle or died along the journey, he has no troops to help him in the upcoming battle. *"My men were thrown in the water, and bobbing like sea crows they were washed away on the running waves all around the black ship, and the god took away their homecoming."* (12.417-419)

Master Of Both Worlds

This is the climax of the narrative. Everything has built up to this point of the story, the final confrontation. Normally, the hero must confront the major antagonist on their own. Most often, this requires the hero to become a martyr for the cause. The hero's powers become fully realized, and having incorporated the lessons from the journey into the normal world, the hero can now use their powers without hindrance. The hero uses their new skills to bring balance to both worlds.

After proving himself to his family, Odysseus enters into the sixteenth stage, Master Of Both Worlds. In this section of the narrative, Odysseus, Penelope and Telemachus create a distraction that allows the hero to face all the suitors at once. The hero sentences them to death by saying, *"You dogs, you never thought I would any more come back from the land of Troy, and because of that you despoiled my household, and forcibly took my serving women to sleep beside you, and sought to win my wife while I was still alive, fearing neither the immortal gods who hold the wide heaven, nor any resentment sprung from men to be yours in the future. Now upon you all the terms of destruction are fastened." (22.35-41)"* and then, *"...all that you have now, and what you could add from elsewhere, even so, I would not stay my hands from the slaughter, until I had taken revenge for all the suitors' transgression. Now the choice has been set before you, either to fight me or run, if any of you can escape death and its spirits. But I think not one man will escape from sheer destruction." (22.62-67)*

Freedom To Live

In this stage, the hero is finally free to return to the normal world. However, something is different about them on the inside. The hero has taken on a new form. They are no longer the old person that clings to their flaw/crutch, but rather reborn. Sometimes this means the hero takes on a new title, position, or station in life. Other times, this means the hero is looked at with respect from those who shunned him before the journey. This is because the hero is the embodiment of the lessons they have learned. They can now go about life free of fear or pain from the old antagonistic force.

After the suitors are dispatched, the story enters the seventeenth and final stage of the Hero's Journey, Freedom To Live. Now that he is home in Ithaca, and doesn't have to contend against any other suitors, Odysseus can finally live as rightful king of Ithaca with his wife Penelope and his son Telemachus. Through his journey he's learned humility and what it truly means to be a king. It's not just an inherited title passed down because of bloodlines. A true king must earn their place on the throne by serving his countrymen, his people, his family and ultimately society.

Recap

As mentioned earlier, the Return Act is the final act of the Hero's Journey and is comprised of six distinct stages. During these stages the hero must return the boon back to the normal world in order to revitalize society. Not all heroes will wish to return to the normal world, and sometimes they may need help getting back. Along their way, they may be chased and they will face many challenges which will culminate in a final climactic confrontation with the major antagonistic force. In order to succeed, the hero will have to make a sacrifice which normally requires them to overcome a major flaw. After defeating the major antagonist, the hero will be free to live in both worlds without fear, as a key member of society.

SELECTED BIBLIOGRAPHY

Campbell, Joseph, Phil Cousineau, and Stuart L. Brown. *The Hero's Journey: The World of Joseph Campbell : Joseph Campbell on His Life and Work*. San Francisco: Harper & Row, 1990. Print.

Homer, , and Robert Fitzgerald. *The Odyssey*. New York: Vintage Books, 1990. Print.

Thank You From Story Ninjas

Story Ninjas Publishing would like to thank you for reading our book. We hope you found value in this product and would love to hear your feedback. Please provide your constructive criticism in a review on Amazon. Also feel free to share this book through the various social media platforms.

Be the first to review the Modern Monomyth: Mythological Storytelling by clicking here.

Other Books by Story Ninjas

Story Ninjas Publishing hopes you enjoyed this book. You can check out our other books here.

About Story Ninjas

Story Ninjas Publishing is an independent book publisher. Our stories range from science fiction to paranormal romance. Our goal is to create stories that are not only entertaining, but endearing. We believe engaging narrative can lead to personal growth. Through unforgettable characters and powerful plot we portray themes that are relevant for today's issues.

You can find more Story Ninja's products here.

Follow Story Ninjas!!!

E-mail: Story-ninjas@story-ninjas.com
Twitter: @StoryNinjas
Youtube: @StoryNinjas
Amazon: Story Ninjas
G+: +Story Ninjas
Facebook: StoryNinjasHQ
LinkedIn: Story-Ninjas
Blogger: Story-NinjasHQ

About The Author

Who Is Josh Coker?

- Josh is known as a premiere writing mentor and consultant, exclusively serving high-fee authors in the book publishing industry. He's known for creating wildly successful story narratives that increase audience engagement while delivering powerful thematic lessons.

- Josh is the author of the Modern Monomyth and several works of fiction, co-founder of Story-Ninjas Publishing, and creator of Reciprocal Narrative Infrastructure, Thematic Resonance and Subconscious Storytelling.

- For the past 15 years, Josh has been writing, publishing and researching fiction. He's helped outline, write, edit, and publish hundreds of stories.

Follow Josh!!!

Email: jcoker@story-ninjas.com

Instagram: @Joshumusprime

Facebook: Josh Coker

YouTube: @Tipperdy

Twitter: @Joshumusprime

LinkedIn: Joshua Coker

Amazon: Josh-Coker